Songs for Sometime Saints

To Barbara, a saint-in-the making,
God bless you.
Love and prayers,
Sister Jean Paul Zagorski, SSND

✦

Songs for Sometime Saints

Jean Paul Zagorski, SSND

Thomas F. Masloski

EDITOR

ISBN: 978-1-4675-9586-5

Songs for Sometime Saints
Author: Zagorski, SSND, Jean Paul

Table of Contents

In Gratitude / xi

Introduction / xiii

1. Songs of God's Good Earth / 1

Sing a Song of the Earth / 2
Spring Garden / 3
Spring Haiku / 4
January Full Moon / 5
Anomaly / 6
February in Wisconsin / 7
March Meditation / 8
Crepe Myrtle / 9
The Night I Saw Heat Lightning / 10
Does the Caterpillar / 12
St. Mary of the Pines, Chatawa / 13
Apples / 14
In Neglect of Nectarines / 15
Blueberry Jam / 16
First Snow of Winter / 18
Creation / 19
Getting Wood / 20

II. Songs of Saints and Sometime Saints / 23

Friends / 24
Fidelity / 25
Sainthood / 26
To One Who Loves / 27
Joan of Arc / 28
John the Baptist / 34
Making Soup / 35
To Dad / 36
To My Photographer Friend / 37
To Sean / 38
Forgiveness / 39
Night Prayer / 40
Someday / 42
Reflection on Ephesians 2: 19-22 / 43

III. Songs of Celebration / 45

Celebration / 46
A Feast of Angels Michael, Gabriel, Raphael / 47
Advent II / 48
After the Angel / 49
Reflection on Annunciation / 50
Breath of the Spirit / 51
Pre-Christmas / 52
First Snow / 53
Bethlehem Blessing / 54
Magi Again / 55
JESUS / 56
Lent / 57
Lenten Survivor / 58
16th Nisan / 59
Magdalen Easter Morning / 60
Scarred God / 61

IV. Songs of Journey and Change / 63

When One Door Closes / 64
The Big Move / 65
Senior Bus ID / 66
Adolescence / 67
Grandma's Poem / 68
Christmas Call (for Mike so soon deceased) / 70
Mother, Post Stroke / 72
Tanka: In Anticipation of a New School Year / 73
Dachau Now / 74
Last Wish / 76
Winter Down / 77
Serendipity / 80
After Beast Cancer / 81
Birthday Blues / 82
Act of Hope / 83
Aged Seasoning / 84
Farewell / 85

V. Songs from the Inside Out / 87

Sarx / 88
Rain Song / 89
Question / 90
October's End / 91
Decision / 92
Dialogue / 93
Autumn Ascetics / 94
Call / 95
Cycling Unseasonably / 96
Prayer from the Pits / 97
Peace on Earth to All of Good Will / 98
No More / 99
Life Insurance / 100
Spring Prayer / 101
Eye Surgery / 102

The Path / 103
Note to My Spiritual Director / 104
Prayer before Partaking in the Liturgy / 105

VI. Alleluia / 107

Give Us This Day / 108
A Prayer for Bits and Pieces / 109
In Hopes of Hatching / 110
Lines in Honor of One Who Loves Me / 111
Of What to Sing in Spring / 112
Love / 113
Lesson in the Labyrinth / 114
Darling, I Am Growing Older / 115
Query / 116
Remembering / 117
Affirmation / 118
Our Journey's Landmarks / 119
Thank You Prayer / 120
Prayer to my Prodigal God / 121
Woman at the Well in Samaria / 122
This Is My Body / 123
Memorial / 124
Short Prayer / 125

Scriptual References in the Poems / 127

In Gratitude

Thanks to the many people who insisted I "write a book." Thanks to Mike Vogel, Bennet McBride, many of my School Sisters of Notre Dame, Pauline Croker, Miriam Rinsler and my cousins. Special thanks to my cousin Tom, who researched the technicalities, managed the project and got help from others in the book publishing business. Special thanks to my Uncle Ray, who helped make the book possible.

Introduction

We all try to be good, but sometimes we slip up.
Let's face it, it's hard to be good all the time. We are
sometime saints. These poems are for all of us and
for specific people. Like the psalms, you will find
a variety of poems—praise poems, gratitude poems,
down-in-the-pits poems, love poems, sorry poems,
wondrous\nature poems. To broaden understanding
of some of them there is a reference to relevant
scripture at the end of the book.

Reflections on Being a Poet

Being a poet is forever being subject to two realities
feeling the tension in my own body so keenly
the only temporary relief is to bind the two together
with careful chiseled words.
Being a poet is being forever apart and pulled
and pulling in to keep my skin in one piece.
Being a poet is never being whole for long
for longing for the earth and heaven
is tearing theologies from the security of muffled meanings
into one clear hope like lightning here and gone.
And if one truth should cloud my vision for a time,
all lapses into rhyme and simple songster stuff
seducing village virgins to some shepherd's tent,
or bells that jingle on some nostalgic sleigh far away.
No, words must clang like heavy hammers on iron nails
fixing world to world until they're somehow one
like blood on wood or slivers in the skin,
mixing joy and pain like wine and water,
life and death like bread and bodies.
Faith and doubt are unsifted out of mystery,
celebrated in the labor of the poet's unborn being.

I.

Songs of God's Good Earth

Sing a Song of the Earth

Sing me a song of the earth, I asked,
and the astronomer did sing
of galaxies of galaxies and
the tiny planet earth.
I did not understand
for I am small
and his was a song of immensity.

Sing me a song of the earth, I asked,
and the geologist did sing
of ages and ages of ages
of slow and constant change.
I did not understand
for I am young
and his was a song of eternities.

Sing me a song of the earth, I asked,
and the geographer did sing
of mountains, of seas, of valleys
and how the people dwell in them.
I liked his song
for it was somewhat a song of peoples.

Sing me a song of the earth, I asked,
and a boy in a tree did sing.
His was the sweetest song
I loved his song, for he sang:
The earth…it is my home.

*S*pring *Garden*

Spring comes in little pockets
between winter's last blasts
and summer's full-throated alleluias.

Sturdy daffodils, known to survive
with toes covered in snow,
stand sentinel until the tall purple irises
take over in the changing of the guard.

3

Spring Haiku

Spring explodes behind
our backs while we bid farewell
to winter's worries.

I get caught in buds
battling bloom between spring's
winter relapses.

January Full Moon

Winter morning moon
full against a slate blue sky
looks cold and lonesome.

Bare branches reach up
to catch winter morning moon
so full and fragile.

Anomaly

In the midst of bitter January
cold enough to bite the heart out,
comes a thaw, and then again the harsh
cold-heartedness that makes the fingers sting.
Find a magnolia tree. Behold the bud,
pale and fuzzy and somehow
secretly full of patience and hope
waiting to proclaim the spring.

*F*ebruary in Wisconsin

Each day's sun sneaks in a bit earlier,
lingers a bit longer.
The observant, careful of ice and mittened for cold,
gather thin slices of hope
for spring.

March Meditation

Do we really know
beneath the snow
which seeds and roots
and bulbs will grow?

Can we tell at all
what died last fall
now sprouts and shoots
at spring's soft call?

Don't we see the face
under icy lace
of life and beauty
in mud and grace?

Crepe Myrtle

Born in secret star pod
fragile pink flower displays
the tender touch of God
before our very eyes.

The Night I Saw Heat Lightning

How like a hill humped in twilight time
the heap of cloud, so sunset brushed and still,
had massed itself against the coming night.
The silent flash and streak of heat-held light,
the white and bursting veins of cloud, coursed through
and through and through to drive it all apart.

It stretched across our hot, hot world, apart
almost, and flashing, ripping all the time
we watched, and was by dark not even through.
When we had put ourselves to bed, it still
was bursting with its crazy slash of light
to be a nervous star protesting night.

Only a few rumbles rumpled our night—
A groan, perhaps, of cloud falling apart,
a something burst by its own broken light
and carried by the wind into a time
to come. Then in the morning all was still.
There was no cloud for dawn to come break through.

The heat had broken, too, a bit. All through
the day a welcome breeze sweet-promised night
to stay and billow soft and cool and still.
No need tonight to tear the bed apart
to hope for one unsweltered moment's time
of sleepfulness before the morning light.

Slight-quartered moon and stars, perhaps to light
the treetop leaves and shyly shimmer through
my silent window, soon will bless the time –
the waited, wondered, weary time of night

when I can let myself fall full apart
like clouds that break on winds and still

are clouds, remade, renewed, reburst and still
at last dissolved in some fantastic light,
sustained in warm, thick air, alone, apart,
and then transformed again to clouds split through
again by currents of some heated night
in other skies and yet another time.

One one-ing Light I pray to come burst through
when I am all apart on that dark night
when all is still and there is end of time.

Does the Caterpillar

Does the caterpillar
understand the cocoon time?
Does it fear the self-entombment
or realize the wrappered womb
the birthing place of butterflies?
Is it aware in its seclusion
with darkness bound around?
Is it awake to the agony of change
or is becoming all benumbed
in blindness?
Does it remember,
or does the pretty winged one
Lethe-like forget in silken sun
its caterpillary?

St. Mary of the Pines, Chatawa

Majestic tall pines anchor the scene—
layered luscious extravagant greens
of flowering bush and hills serene
and sweet gums feigning stars for leaves.

Apples

Perhaps apples are
the first healthy fast food straight
from the hand of God.

*I*n *Neglect of Nectarines*

I confess ignoring the nectarine
in favor of the deep pink of watermelon
sweetly steeped in the memory of childhood
with rind reaching ear to ear,
best eaten outdoors and spitting seeds
at siblings four feet away.

I confess neglecting the nectarine
for the lure of big, bright strawberries
while remembering the rewarding flavor
of the tiny wild ones we patiently picked
in small handfuls before breakfast from the plot
between the driveway and the woods.

I confess passing over the nectarine
for the victor's booty of juicy red raspberries,
plucked in battle while armored in jean-jacket,
camouflaged in bandana and bug spray to protect
from tiny thorns in too close bushes and occasional
sparring with mosquitoes, wasps and bees.

But one day the nectarine, with its precious gold
wrapped in royal ripeness, won me with suspect softness,
willingly releasing its flesh from its pit and letting
its life dribble down my fingers, proving itself
a noble partner with red things proclaiming
summer's sweetness and bounty.

*B*lueberry Jam

Frost crimples crisp-curled fallen leaves
and a white card in the window
with big black letters reads:

JAM SESSION SUNDAY

Three-thirty a little man
bounces at the piano
playing snatches and catches
of this and that
with variations.

A bass at four
warms it up a little.

A short black beard
bellows: "I'll be back—
goin' home to get a drum."

Deep-bottomed laughs
punctuate
round-topped whispers
over clink of ice and glasses—
smoke and crowd
both
hot and thick.

A sax is swing-singing
to the thoomp-thoomp bass
and a red hot trumpet.
The little man at the piano
bounces still.
And the sound is red and yellow.

Knocking six,
and black beard's back
with a beat and a brush
to hush across the cymbals.
At six and seven the hot stuff cools.
Piano man goes one-handed with a ham-on -rye.

The crowd thins.

By eight and nine the guys on the stand
are way out blue and purple.

Thoomp-thoomp bass—
warm brass blows cool.
Black beard keeps the beat
with brush and cymbals.
Piano man is haggard
with a hint of heaven in his half-shut eyes.

The guys on the stand are oblivion.

Hours hang heavy like loose grapes
and fall unnoticed
'til two and a telephone ring—
"Hey, your wife wants to know,
are you coming home?"

Drumsticks slash a cymbal crash
and little black beard
takes his drums and goes.

And silence breaks it up 'til
a colder frost and a white card
reads in big black letters:

JAM SESSION SUNDAY

*F*irst Snow of *W*inter

A little gasp of breathless joy
greets the first snow of winter
clinging to trees, signs and fences,
becoming and beautiful.

Becoming and beautiful,
blinding the eye that beholds it,
snow hides the dying beneath
which we willingly let go.

We willingly let go
of autumnal glory past its prime,
dead and decaying victim of time
covered with snow.

Until, covered with snow,
spring's great thrust begins again
through mud in sprouts of green
with a little gasp of breathless joy.

Creation

All God's love burst forth
Birthing bits of being blest
Being bonded more not less

Getting Wood

Maggie, not quite old but no longer young,
thin, weathered, and a little bent,
goes to get wood.
I go along.
A varied color pieced string
ties ax and saw to her plastic sled.

We walk the frozen river
five feet thick with ice
searching for snow patch footholds
on its slick surface.
We stop to study the cracks
and air bubble patterns
that show ice depth.

She shows me where the good ice is
to chop for drinking water
and wishes for her buckets.
"Another day," we say,
and head for a line of willows
on the far bank of the Yukon River.
The wind blows us backward several times
before we reach it.
The wind doesn't bite so bad
in the opening between the willows.
Not today.

A mile more beyond the opening
we enter another thicket of willows.
There's a spot where Maggie
has stashed some thin logs.
We saw those into two-foot lengths

and look for other likely limbs
as thick as arms or legs.

A load of wood on the sled,
a pile to return to "another time,"
and we are warmed and winded now
finally admitting we are tired.

One more leisurely look
through the thicket
for growths on trunks.
"Punk we use for snuff,"
Maggie grins as she cuts her prize
and stuffs it in her kuspuk pocket.

Even heavily laden
the sled slides easily over the river ice.
The sun is not as warm.
Our steps are slower.
The wind bites harder.

II.

Songs of Saints and Sometime Saints

Friends

O my friends,
you are deep rivers.
You have caverned my heart.
You have sprung wells in my desert.

𝓕idelity

The borders of duty are worn away.
Everyday love extends the limits
planting little surprises
past the expected.
The early days were marked
with deaths and doggedness,
but grace has oiled smooth
the movements now.
The cost is hidden
even from the heart that pays it.

Sainthood

"Vatican strategy on turning popes into saints: When moving a controversial pope along the path, bundle him with a more popular pontiff—the PR calculation apparently being that acclaim for the latter may drown out negative reaction to the former."

NCR "BUNDLING SAINTHOOD" JAN. 8, 2010

What does it take to make a saint?
How beatify someone who ain't?
Pick two: One good, one bad.
The coupling at first seems sad.
But that's, perhaps, how we really do it.
The fiercely good pull the mediocre through it.
We know, of course, saints aren't free from sin,
but God does change us from within.
Keep the good one, throw the bad one out?
Only God knows who's who without a doubt.
St. Augustine, Mary Magdalene, both were sinners
'til repentance and prayer made both winners.

The lesson is to keep on trying.
Make the change before you're dying.
Our loving God will surely take you.
It was with hope and love that God did make you.

To One Who *Loves*

Because of your ever loving amiability
you will frequently
(perhaps constantly)
find yourself in hot water.
But fear not …
love got St. John in a pot of boiling oil
from which he proceeded
little worse for wear.
Love put the heat on St. Joan
(with less fortunate results, alas!)
And St. Paul simply
lost his head to Love.
Peter was turned head over heels,
Lawrence was grilled,
Pere Jogues was quite
devoured with love.
And all because a Man
(named the Son of God)
stretched out His arms in bloody embrace
and cried, "I thirst…"

Joan of Arc

Little shepherdess, go back
to your fields and your sheep.
Go back and dream your dreams,
don't prattle them here.

Peasant maid, sweet shepherdess,
was it only dreams?
I have heard of
a shepherd in a far-off land,
who in the field by a burning bush
stood barefoot
talking to his God.
He led a captive people
from out of Pharaoh's land
through the forty year wilderness
into a Promise.

Yes, young shepherdess,
go back to your sheep.
Go back and once more hear
the Voices.

They are urging:
On to Vaucouleurs
and Dauphin Charles.
On to Orleans
and victory.
On to Rheims
and the kinging of a prince.

An army will not march,
O maid of Lorraine,
at a woman's word.

But the scoffers and protesters
refuse no longer.
The lily on your banner, maid,
the lily, it is you
and more,
virgin warrior.

O shepherdess,
the armor bites and bruises
one used to only wool
and leather.
The saddle is an aching throne
for one who hardly sat
but on the earth
and hearth bench.

But I have heard of
a shepherd tending flocks
within the Promise,
harping and singing songs,
and slinging stones at lions.
Loving a nation
he stoned a giant
and praising God
became a king.

Orleans is won
and, shepherdess,
is there not a glory in leading
a flock of militaire
to victory
and a crown?

The glory you do not claim,
good shepherdess.

Yours only is longing
for home again and fields
full of sheep,
not armor.
O peasant maid, your heart
lies at the hearth in Domremy.

Oh to throw off
aching breastplate,
to cast down
sword and shield
for a valley in Lorraine
and a new-born lamb in the lap!
The crown is won.
Is there no rest for a weary warrior?

And now, young virgin victor,
do the Voices urge
on to Compiegne
and capture,
on to Rouen,
an ending?

Child of the Church,
what are its scholars shouting?
God has laid victory on your sword,
virgin warrior,
and they cry "Witch!"
A vision and a voice
God has given as guide,
young shepherdess,
and they harangue you, "Heretic!"
A tempest for a testing,
dear faithful one,
as they title you, " Apostate!"

Why do you fear
the final battle
fought for blood and banner
different from the ones you've warred
on France's fields?
O militaire,
advance is not asked here,

to hold fast is success,
retreat is sore defeat.
Be strong, French maid.

A prison for a peasant girl
whose only bars
were earth and sky—
a feeble candle
for one who dwelt with blazing sun
and stars.
Be strong French maid.

I have heard of
a Shepherd Who for His flock
became a Lamb and slain
that He might be
both pastor
and pasture
feeding all His gathered lambs
and shepherding His sheep.

And you, little shepherdess,
you are a lamb of His.
Be brave, virgin warrior, in this
last battle.

Where are your soldiers now?
Where is the King
whose crown you won?
And the Voices,
do they comfort you
chained to the stake
knee deep in kindling –
(wood enough for a winter
at Domremy's hearth!)

Where are those who marched
with you,
warrior witch,
humble heretic,
apostate all afraid!

Be brave, French maid.
A cross, O man of God, a cross—
a cross for the virgin warrior.
A winter's fuel
burns hot and high.
Do not fear, sweet shepherdess,
hold fast, hold fast.

And from the flames
a voice,
the peasant maid.
A cry—
a name,
the Shepherd's Name!
He has gathered up His lamb.

Executioner, why do you kneel
and weep in charred wood?
The heart is whole—
A heart unburnt
for all the flame within.

Domremy, your daughter is dead.
Lorraine, you have lost your lamb.
France, your fleur is plucked
and planted in a fairer valley.

O France,
your young men dream no dreams,
your old men see no visions.
A shepherd maid has heard a Voice
and heeded.

John the Baptist

This is the month of first-frost days and skinny trees,
of days bright as long-gone leaves,
gray as death cold seas.
This is the time of the lone bird crying,
of the squirrel and the lumbering bear.
It is the season of the short sun,
the silver night of the long moon.
These are the hours that slow into stillness,
the quiet of sleep....
                          the silence of death
broken by the cold clear cry of the desert dweller,
the long lean prophet awaking leaden ears!
Truth is burnt across his face.
Lyric joy is on his tongue.
Desire splits his lips in song
of a Silent One beneath the ice.

Quiet as the Promised Peace,
we pray in the night of frozen plains
lit by the bright-boned singer in camel cloth,
and wait the Birthing Prophesied.

Making Soup

Pocketed away in a humble convent
in the high-class fast-paced east side of Milwaukee
is a former Alaskan missioner
making soup from turkey bones
salvaged from Thanksgiving dinner,
boiling them long, then pulling them
from the inviting stock and stripping them clean,
cherishing the values learned from her Yup'ik teachers:
it is responsibility and respect for the bird
that gave its life to feed our hunger.

This is an all day thing – this making soup.
Warm smells begin to fill the kitchen.
With hungry patience she washes, peels, chops
carrots, celery, onion, even leaves of the giant cabbage
her uncle brought from a friend's farm.
She slides them gently, expectantly, in the boiling pot.
Later she'll add tomatoes for color.

Willing to share this elixir of life, she will offer it to
friends.
Some she knows will decline, preferring something
from familiar cans with red and white labels.
It doesn't matter. She has this treasure
to warm next week's winter days.

To Dad

Could I have chosen
of all fathers
none would have suited

but your gentleness
that nestles birds
of sweet wild dreams
and hopes like fresh June strawberries
cherished in their own
flavored rarity.

Could I have chosen
of all fathers
none would have suited

but the intensity
of your conviction
like the horse at the Derby gate
reined in for power,
conserved for the back-stretch miracle
where, in the final analysis,
all things count upon their essence.

To My Photographer Friend

ON SEEING THINGS DIFFERENTLY

Perceptive one catching paradoxes
in your box,
you find wonder and capitalize
on mysteries in old men's perplexed eyes,
pick life's parts separate
and simple
and all alone elegant.
A fountain's wet and water
is a way of life.
Make time stand still and last week's hour
is present for all posterity.

*T*o *Sean*

I want to dance on still blue air.
What's it like to sing
strings of hope through the body's longing?

*F*orgiveness

I can't fault Eve for picking that apple—
shiny red and firm, crisp and juicy,
slightly tart, yet sweet.
Such potential in that orb,
(though she might not have known.)

Night Prayer
(REFLECTION ON JOHN CHAPTER 6)

Bread of Life, you speak of living, never dying,
eternal life and rising.
I don't know how to believe it.
Belief is such a fragile thing –
one step up from fairy tale,
a whole world away from any way of knowing.

The ones I loved have died
and risen (I hope) on some other side
of a realm I cannot touch.
Their memories cheer and haunt my prayers.
 I want so much to feel their real love again.

And now my Mom who has lived through sorrow
slowly dies in sadder sorrow still.
We eat your flesh and drink your blood.
Our hunger drove us to you:
hunger for one whose love is real
and does not use, abuse, exploit—
hunger for someone whose care can
make a difference.

My belief has ridden its fairy tale horse
to the furthest edge.
I don't know how to pray today:
that we may die so we can really live,
or really live throughout our dying?

Mom and I are praying. I am crying.
A fragile faith sincerely says the words you taught.

We pray: "Give us this day…."
Mother's words are jumbled.
You know the intent of what is said.
"Give us this day our daily bread."

Someday

Someday He will
wait upon my shores with words of peace
and my bones will forget
the cold and wet of the night's long watch
and only know
the glow of fire
and friend
and food.

Reflection on Ephesians 2-19-22

You are aliens and strangers no longer,
but God's family and household members.
The bonds are lasting and stronger
afire with the Spirit's own embers.

Gathered together as One,
not thatch or sticks or sod,
aligned with Jesus the Son
strong bricks for the dwelling of God.

III.

Songs of
Celebration

Celebration

There is, at any point in my time, cause enough
if I will see it, to celebrate:
one gold leaf against a mute gray sky;
a bird that pecks at seeds in my back yard;
you who live with me, yearning
in your silent hope and private dreams.

To celebrate—
not in ritual nor sense of duty—
compelled by sense of love (however slim and tenuous)
to be responsive, wordless at times,
tearful at times in my own terror and hope
...there is cause enough.

There is cause enough to celebrate
what is fragile and persistent,
in spite of my own winter and thunderous storms
and ice-bone cold,
declaring all that is not spring and summer
is preparation for it.

I celebrate
the inch by inch assent
(like glaciers receding)
of momentary conversion.

$\mathcal{A}$ Feast of Angels Michael, Gabriel, Raphael

Angel—not winged creature of the holy card,
not weaponed sentry standing guard,
but heavenly spirit protecting
what is good upon our earth—
particular and pervasive spirit
releasing the power of goodness
that persists through bad times.

Angel—not ethereal messenger boy,
not limited literal telegram,
but voiced spirit of our listening
to the good within and without—
the rush of wisdom previously unheeded,
the confidence (gift of God) now needed.

Angel—not mysterious map bearer,
not BC triple A,
but loving presence with us on the way—
mentors seeking nothing for themselves,
pilgrim partners bringing presence
to the struggles and the joys of journey.

We can name them as we wish:
Michael, Gabriel, Raphael, gift of God,
or humanity transcending itself.

Advent 11

When the leaf's gone gold
and berries blood the bush,
when the wind bursts clouds from inside out,
inside my bones I know
the cry from frozen rippled sands
to all the empty spaces half-known 'til now in me.
All the urgencies are born again;
impatience frames the flesh to fitness
for the wonder-wrapped announcement:

NOW!

When shivered-thin and silvered trees
grown gaunt stand sentinel,
when frost hewn world signals all the want
and need of whom we wait,
impatience learns the pain of perseverance.
Eager becomes endure how
all the holes have grown
in expectation.

After the Angel

I have a secret.
Shall I whisper it in the wind?
Shall I shout it to the stars?
I have a secret.
It will burst my breast
for want of one
to help me hold it.

Lullaby low, lullaby…
Shall I soften it with singing?
Shall I cry
and ease it all with joyful tears
like the weeping willow?
Lullaby, lullaby low…

I have a secret
and how can I hold it?
Or understand it all?
Or understand it…

Reflection on Annunciation

It was not with words of Angels
that you bid us be for you
a place to let your Word grow
to let our life be His.
(Or is it the other way around?)

Our yes is maybe much more slow,
and sometimes bordering on no,
but quite indefinite.
You accept it anyway
and send us off to needy cousins
and home again to questions
while the answer grows within.

Breath of the Spirit

There are no familiar patterns
in what wind has done.
When God breathes,
the never before is now.

Pre-Christmas

Soft pink silences there are,
like a lullaby gone asleep …
sweet white silences
of snow and humble things
like folded wings of doves.
And there is the silence
of a Child in the womb.

First Snow

Times are my thoughts have turned to snow—and white
is sprinkled free among a darkened wood
to happify and change, like none else could,
a somber empty day to wondered night.
Old eyes grow young from youngness of the sight,
and virtue's root is grown from nature's good.
Now cleansed I stand where once I soiled stood,
now once more simpled in the snow-shone light.
And thoughts are come to me about a why,
the why a child had come long years ago,
the incarnate God, to suffer and to die
to let his life and love, like rivers, flow
across our dark and barren winter sky
and come to scatter grace like stars and snow.

Bethlehem Blessing

I am a shepherd.
My life is tedium and mystery.
My thoughts are grass and water
and the safety of the flock.
Wind and sun and weather and wild creatures
move me to gratitude and fear.
A gentle breeze on sunny days
brings songs of praise.
Wind-chill and ice freeze my brain
to prayers for survival of the moment.
Nights are full of fear and wonder.
My ears sort sounds into bleats,
heartbeats, breaths, and things
among the bushes.
My eyes strain to see into the dark,
catch glimpses of eyes and movements,
and gaze at stars and marvel.
Like **that** night.
A bright whirlwind of angels?
Words too wondrous to fathom
and off we go to experience mystery
and history firsthand.
I do not understand or try to teach.
I only live the life within my reach.
I am a shepherd.

Magi Again

Let us celebrate the wisdom
that took slight signs
to heart and head and hope.
Let us celebrate the wisdom
that made minds wrestle
with the puzzle of Promise
almost lost in too long times of trial
and much too many words.
Let us celebrate the wisdom
that let us move in faith
through dark nights and deserts
and humbly to Him.

JESUS

Just because, he loves us,
Each and every one,
Surely, truly,
Unconditionally,
Sweetly.

*L*ent

This moment of grace
is stuck in our face
want it or not—
a call to a leanness,
to abandon all meanness,
to love life a lot.

Our wise Mother Church
goes on a search
for the goodness forgot
amid burdens we're bearing
that stifle our caring
to diddly squat.

Come hear the readings,
the sincerest of pleadings
to stop what we're doing and start
to enter within,
acknowledge the sin
in the mind and the heart.

Lent does its thing
to drag us to spring
through cold, ice and snow.
We walk the Way,
relearn to pray
and again come to know

the God who can reach us,
the God who can teach us
and make all things new.
It's then in the greening
we find our true meaning
and God's face in you.

Lenten Survivor

With spirit weary of winter darkness
and cold gripping at the heart
like the hand of death,
with Christmas and its glitter gone,
blackened snow piled along our lives,
even the heaviness of coats and boots
become a burden like Lenten purple
and crosses shouldered.
The evening news with its daily dose spews
deadly disasters from the earth, winds and waters,
shootings on our streets, the young abused,
or their bodies shattered on our highways
or gathered up in bits from battlefields.
On all this I surreally superimpose
the Way of the Cross.
My soul and mind struggle with the paradox
of love and death and life.
(Too often it looks like death is winning.
God, I hope I'm wrong!)
I surreptitiously gulp facefuls of sunshine
between gray sheets of rain,
peer into muddy patches
for the least bit of green poking through.

16th Nisan

Dead like winter-went
we were until one sprout spring
You Eastered in us

Magdalen Easter Morning
(REFLECTION ON JOHN 20: 11-18)

I know more of tears and empty tombs
than of a gardener God.
The echo of nails and soul wrenching weeping
dulls my ears to the sound
of my name spoken softly
on a solemn Sunday morning.
The resurrection hasn't yet
aroused me from my grieving.
Though dawn has cracked the horizon open,
it has not broken my nighttime shell
of searching through what I've known,
nor allowed me to lay hold of the unimaginable.

Scarred God

Come look, and hold my hands.
No, they're not raw and gross and bloody.
They've healed. Lumpy welts remain
that can be felt and traced quite easily.
There is no present pain,
but I can remember it as real as yesterday,
even after these almost two thousand years.
(At times, memories still are wet with tears.)
My Father asked if he should smooth
these scars away. I told him, no.
They are my credentials to console
the suffering ones who come.
They grab my hand and know I know.
We don't need to search for words.
Those whom sorrow's almost rent,
I hold close. They've felt my side
and often cried from sheer relief
to know their God can know their grief.

If my body were as perfect as the day
my Mother gave me flesh,
there'd be nothing there to save the tenuous faith
of those who find divinity too distant.
But scars of their human-God help them claim
their kingdom roots, their holy name.

IV.

Songs of Journey and Change

When One Door Closes

When one door closes
and for a time such as getting used to takes
I must walk in shadow,

let me remember
if there is a door for keeping out,
there's a somewhere door for letting in.

The Big Move

On Friday
the movers came to carry away
the basement things: billions of boxes
(some even marked!), exercise machines,
tables, chairs, washer, dryer,
desks, rolled rugs, dehumidifiers—
the works whisked away
in less than two hours as if it were easy.
The barrenness, the great empty,
starkly simple remains.

On Saturday
the whole house empties in three hours.
The movers, like army ants,
methodically march through.
The muscled men don't mind huge or heavy.
I, in frozen awe, stay out of the way.
Ten years of life pass before my eyes.

Senior Bus ID

Look here. There you have it
for all the world to see—
proof of aging and haggardness.
Not even I can deny it's me.

It was a rather hurried situation
and attempted beautification
never even entered my mind
before going to the station.
I had a ride and time enough
to squeeze in registration.
I had brought along all
required documentation.

I was thinking only of necessity
of this official pictured bus ID
qualifying me for a half-fare ticket.
I never planned on looking wicked!

After trim and styling mid next week,
I'll board the bus looking pretty chic.
Are bus drivers trained to see
the picture and I are really me?
Do they even have the time to care
if pass and person really square?

*A*dolescence

Rain washed branches bow
in springtime suntime noonday.
Buoyant blossoms burst.

Grandma's Poem

Grandma's poem isn't finished yet.
It's in the deep down feelings
that lap a memory's shore.
The words haven't found their ways yet
for the faith she simply lived.

I remember some years ago
waiting with Grandma for Jesus' First Friday visit.
She progressed through pages of her Polish prayer book
chock full of holy pictures—remembrances mostly
of friends and family who had preceded her
to Jesus.
She paused with many thoughts
at the picture of St. Ann.
"Jesus' Grandma," she explained
and simply shared that faith
that made her such a good Grandma.

I saw so many times
that wordless pondering of things
she did not understand, but held in holy hands
before her Lord.
She had faith enough for all her family.

I am privileged to be her grandchild,
for to be such is to be special.
Anything we could accomplish
was so celebrated in her heart.
We were heroes and miracle workers—
if for no one else, we were in Grandma's eyes.
Her love, her pride made us special.

Grandma's poem isn't finished yet.
Its rhythms are beating in our blood,
Its words are finding forms in our flesh.
Grandma's poem isn't finished yet.

Christmas Call
(FOR MIKE SO SOON DECEASED)

I called to say hello.
I did not know
it would also be good-by.
You said you were watching
green grass grow.
(It should be snow!)
On to global warming and ozone holes
causing krill to die.
No more fish food,
no more fish.
Fisheries failing
(as was your health.)
You hoped to hang on two more years,
get help from Medicare and live
happy ever after.

It's not that easy, I remarked,
and you embarked upon another
theme of institutional injustice.
You raged about hurt heaped
upon a gentle soul you'd met
undone by faithfulness to faith betrayed.
We both knew
such to be true.

Had I read this book
authored by a Canadian theologian?
(Ha! Your Agnosticism's flawed!
You who profess not to be religious!)

You, in your scientific bent,
meant to prove your lost ideal God
and diligently searched for truth,
denying and defying,
picking apart all being and perception.
Then measurably
recreated it.

(God laughed and led you on.
You his son, yet feeling orphaned.)
Now you know:
Love isn't in the brain nor in the body,
but in the soul.

Mother, Post Stroke

Mom hasn't lost her mind,
only half her body
and the words and thoughts
get trapped within
the parts that will not work.

Whole worlds of "want to tell you"
linger beyond the lost look she sometimes
drifts behind,
her mind trying to find its way
to say her love, her need, her hurts,
her broken dreams.

It seems so sad and yet quite wondrous
that those feelings she was slow
to show no longer blocked by words
now flow so freely.
A hug, a tug will speak her love
or urgency. Her eyes caress me
with concern. A grunt or push
of impatience tells me I had better hurry
or soothe away frustration mounting.
But best I love the belly laugh
that tells how well the half
that works is working.

*T*anka: *In Anticipation of a New School Year*

Hungry little birds
waiting so expectantly what you do not know,
trusting—please keep on trusting.
Then perhaps I, too, will grow.

Dachau Now

Is there no forgiveness ever here
in this land of beauty, in this camp of stone
where sin raged strong?
Is there no forgiveness ever
for this people who lived near
this hidden sin,
who pulled it deep within
when gates were sprung
and grieved for lifetimes
carrying shame within the name
of Dachau?
The soil has long ago soaked up the sorrow
so many bodies shed.
Winds have mercifully dispersed on years of time
the stench that choked the soul.
There remains this monument to sin
so we won't forget to what degree
we are capable of unlove.

Is there no forgiveness ever
for the hands that did, the lips that let
the deeds be done here?
Is there no forgiveness ever even in conversion
and lives long quietly, silently turned about?
And what about the torture of those souls
     for forty years?
Are they not human too?
Is there no forgiveness ever?

If there is no forgiveness ever
for thousands slain, repented,
can there be forgiveness even

for centuries of daily sin one-on-one:
the cutting word that strips a soul of dignity;
rejection that shrivels one as sure as lack of bread;
indifference that snuffs the light of life
one candle at a time until the night of nothingness
    takes over;
violence and abuse that takes its pound of flesh
and soul from those who'll not be whole again
this side of heaven?
Are guilt and shame another name
for humanity?
(I seek no excuse, just the possibility with conversion
to reclaim the heritage once given with our image.)

If there's no forgiveness here at Dachau,
if guilt is grown forever in the blood of those
who lived and live here,
there's no forgiveness anywhere for anyone
who has sinned against a brother or a sister
of any creed or color.
And blood still screams from Abel on
and Christ has died in vain.

But somewhere caught between our earth and heaven
in God-man's pain a Word's been given.
One garden spot, one hill
stand witness still
to sweat and tears and blood poured out
and the quiet shout for hearts rent in sorrow—
"Father, forgive them...."

Last Wish

Take me to the window,
I want to watch it snow
and let the pieces of my life go
and fall together on the ground.
I've loved all the little bits,
but I need to see how it fits
together....Take me to the window.
I need to watch it snow.

Winter Down

I

Rain gray
has been eased a bit
by snow white—
just a tad—
touching that empty space
that turns my face to
too tired to live.

I reach the place
where poets meet
warmly welcomed,
but no one's here
in the empty white room
surgically barren
like my soul.
Why'd I come?
There's stuff to do at home,
but I don't want to.
I don't want to anything
these days,
these weeks,
these months.
I hope briefly this white room
will become the womb
of life that grabs my soul.

Let go of work, of duty.
Plant little seeds of beauty
hidden in the gray of despair.
Let green grow there.

Let sunshine sing
or let the gray grow black
and beautiful in its depth
and death.

But know I faced the space
honest and true.

II

It's good to share the pain
and hear it leave me
like a sigh,
each breath following
the other like the hands
of a masseuse soothing
the stress from the skin,
from each muscle,
going deeper and deeper
right down to the bone.

It's good to share the pain
acknowledging the real
and letting it go
a little bit more each time.

It's good to share the pain
and peel it off like dirty bandages
that mummified it into
some palpable mystery
that I forgot somewhere
and carried around
just because.

I forgot and now
the dust, layer after layer,
is more real than the mystery.

It's good to share the pain,
each word like rain
washing away the dust,

soaking through the bandages,
dissolving the mystery
to manageable muck
to be scraped away
until no more.

It's good to share the pain,
word by word slowly named,
renamed, until the power's
gone.

Serendipity

Summer sends the child reeling—
picnics, pools, parades,
barefoot, boisterous, ball-playing,
biking, picking berries,
bouncing down sidewalks,
flopping on green grass
and daring daydreams
of ice cream midday!

After Breast Cancer

Here's to all the zero-breasted,
single-breasted women
and those who gave a pound of flesh
more or less.

We've faced the knife,
dreaded chemo, radiation,
and medication for life.
But that's the key—
for life, for LIFE!

Birthday Blues

It's your birthday and you're not here—
haven't been for three years now.
Your absence makes me face my own mortality.
Can't say I fear it. It's just depressing.
In the greater scheme of things
it's small, but when I'm alone
it looms like King Kong
climbing through the city of my soul.
The undone and disorder haunt me.
Ideals lay like shattered crystals at my feet.
In the dark of night each moment seems
too short for change, and daytime
tosses tons of distractions on the path.
Their screaming urgencies overwhelm me
into paralysis. Dismissing endings
is the only way to cope. Each minute
begins again another now and now and now
to face the first in front of me and do in hope.

Act of Hope

Falling apart now
so fast, unexpectedly,
nothing left to grasp.

Who would have believed
fatigue and fear are stronger
than touted love?

Going through motions
of work and prayer and caring,
hoping it matters,

if not now, somewhere
in the course of my own time
or someone else's.

Aged Seasoning

I might blame it on global warming,
this phenomenon of not knowing
where we are in the year.

Perhaps it's really change of career
that has little or no breaks, no variance.
Holidays slip by so swiftly,
no "school's out" relief to anticipate.
Or maybe it's true about how time passes
more quickly as you age, just when you need it most.
No one says it out loud, no billboards proclaim it,
but deep down inside we know "The end is nigh."

*F*arewell

Friends grow old and die.
Life is still and gray. I cry,
feel lost and empty.

V.

Songs from the Inside Out

Sarx

The flesh is willing but the spirit weak.

I think it died here and there,
bit by bit like the Biafran young,
but surely.
No swift Herod's sword,
no Rachel to weep me—
that supposes love.
(Someday there may be heard a whimper at the Wall.)

There is purity in snow.
I come as freezing rain
that clings to a frozen earth.
I am night without a star to save me.
I am barter for cheap goods—
not changed, exchanged.

I am a sepulcher with no one
to roll away the rock.
I am the howl tangled in the bare branches of faith.

Who shall free me from this death?
Where is He now?

Rain Song

All day and the night before,
the warm thickens and mounds,
full, heavy.

> Heavy is the heart in me.

The little creatures noise so loud,
so anxiously announce

> Could I announce to one

the clouds rolled up against the trees
and threatening—

> sorrow mounded?

now break in streams to splatter-slash
the roofs and walls and windows,

> Being full

to fill up everything and spill over,
find and flood each dry corner
of the deepest earth.

> I shall close my window.

?

Down what bright green street must I walk
to find you, Love?
I've planted a million little seeds of hope,
but they've all come up gray.

October's End

The garden, cut back and weeded,
looks ragged like my soul.
Spring's dreams are tucked away
where I can't see them now.

Decision

Piercing wintery day
clinging between white and gray—
maybe snow or rain.
My soul hangs between
"yes" and "hope" and lets it lay
in hands not its own.

Dialogue

Armed with nothing but my me
into battle going
bravely like a child unaware,
yet cautious, knowing
I will hurt,
be hurt there
in the open place where air
is warmer than my love,
colder than my justice …
Into the open place going
to be opened,
to open out,
by the, to the tender terrifying,
the uncertain hoped,
the barely barred—"Come over,
come over—let
Love…."

Autumn Ascetics

God of the gold leaf
in the midst of the gloom around me,
you attract something inside me
that holds fragile hope.

God of the blood-red bush,
you call me to cast off shoes
and all that binds me, holds me back
from the risk of consummation.

God of the cold gray sky and ice gray waters,
you force autumnal asceticism
to look within and touch an emptiness
that makes me want to run or hide in holes,
yet urges me desperately to reach out.

God of the seasonal grace gift
that voices gratitude
in spite of my ever-shrinking circles,
you let me stand in nothingness
with uneasy comfort and confusion,
but confident in your love.

God of frozen white wind,
you hollow me out for waiting—
hungry, hopeful waiting—
and wonder.

C_{all}

Wash soft the rocks upon my brittle shore,
naked, skeletally fragile in your presence.
Whisper. Let your word wind in the womb of my brain.
Let me be ...

> Sun whiten me, chase out
> the night that claims my bones.

Oh, your joys are little glass bells
upon the rocks I dare not reach
until your waves pull back
and tell me come.

Cycling Unseasonably

In these fifty days of Easter season,
as the church proclaims the glorious
mysteries of resurrection, and ascension,
and descent of the Spirit
with blessing and mission,
life doesn't match.

Betrayal in dark spring gardens,
accusations and stripping
and nailing to dragged wood,
the glory has seeped out and
slid back into a sorrowful decade:
physical agony and loneliness in choice.
.

"What is truth?" is perceived
too personally to be unmistakable.
Power is too heady to be reasonable
pushing changes most unseasonal
with cause too thin
to live within.

Ordinary time has become
extraordinarily filled with tears
and fears of figures moving in the dark
we thought we knew, but who did really?
Hearts are shaken.

But didn't slivered dawn and quaking
accompany the Great Awaking
and precede the surge of courage
in fishermen's amazing transformation?

*P*rayer from the *P*its

Why is it my soul takes on the season
of November dreary, dark and cold?
It takes determination
to just get up and do the daily tasks
that in the gray seem empty of significance.

O God! Today is only dry, dark cracks
full of heavy emptiness and disappointments.
Is it just because it's Advent here again?
A year's slipped by with little to show.
Death confronts me nose to nose, and that great Birth
is hiding in the wings beyond my sight.

Show me, O God, into which hole to drop
that faithful hook to catch a bit of hope
to heal my hardened human heart.

Peace on Earth to All of Good Will

If we have not peace, let's check our measure of Good
Will.
To what degree do we have Scroogeosity or Grinchiness?
How strong is our miserliness, how rooted our envy?
How tightly do we cling to our pile of things,
our roles, our point of view, our ways of doing things?
How open are we to strangers, to different ideas,
to cultures other than ours?
Could we learn from nighttime visions,
voices from the dead, or emptiness of heart
amid another's pure joy?
How open are we to the Spirit to change us?
Do we hold God to our own terms?
Can we love without strings?
Can we risk the words of a simple maid
or mean the fateful phrase of a trusting Son?
"Let it be." "Thy will be done."

*N*o *More*

There is no more
to be said for war
but bloodied broken bodies,
lost lives littered for a leader's
greed and lust for power.

There is no more
to be said for war
but hungry children
maimed and orphaned
and empty-eyed except for fear.

There is no more
to be said for war
but heartless, heinous crimes
that rob the souls of those who
do, or see, or hear.

There is no more
to be said for war—
perhaps a bit of honor for loyalty
perhaps a bit of perseverance for surviving—
but
for what?

I've never heard a bird
sing for it.
I've never seen clear waters
wash it away.

*L*ife *Insurance*

Just what is it you are trying to sell?
A guaranteed casket and a hole to put it in?
Comfort for my loved ones
who will have preceded me?
I've not much stake in it.

How about life assurance?
Can you assure me that I'll live it well
for those around me?
Can you assure it will be true
to the God who gave it freely?
Can you assure justice to the end
and mercy all throughout?

Don't sell me a pretty box or a marble drawer
(waterproof and airtight at that! God forbid!)
Let life-giving water wash away
this handful of carbon.
Let gusts of air stir photons of light
into union with the universe
and the Intelligence behind the great design.

Spring Prayer

Was this really March? Some rain, some snow,
daring daffodils and crocuses start to grow
so tall and green and buds are seen
undaunted by ferocious winds that blow.

If only I could that confident be
to ignore the things that threaten me,
to look inside and not to hide
the Son that grows and sets me free.

*E*ye Surgery

It might not work the way it should.
I could lose my sight for good.
Think: less fearsome risk, more hopeful chance.

It's hard to realize
my eyes are not my eyes
but technology's wondrous lens implants.

I see what I have never seen,
the smallest lines on the doctor's screen.
It makes me want to sing and dance!

The $Path$

The path is narrow for decision from within—
without walls, without pressure.
Warning: Abandoning the way
can lead to chaos or self-destruction
like a planet falling out of orbit.
Fortunately, for us, this is not
irredeemable.
Love energy from the Center
can gather the pieces
into something new.

Note to My Spiritual Director

You ask, "How are you with God today?"
Will you understand if I say,
"It's all sunny days and nights
full of moon and bright stars.
I want to sing and dance
flowing with fullness knowing all is gift."
Or "It's a month when days are gray
and nights are clouded with sameness
(like my head) going nowhere.
My innards are heavy as stone
like waiting for a train I think I missed
or it never came....disconnected all the same."
Will you understand the pain of distance
or the patient, but numbing, wait
of a hope I cannot name?

Dear Director, are you OK with my swing of things—
the rush of love or tiny droplets on a string?
You ask, but I have no words
(and little understanding),
only images to give you.
What will you do?

Prayer before Partaking in the Liturgy

Pour out, O God,
pour out your Word through the fibers of my flesh.
Let my bones thunder in your strength.
Sing your song in me, let it stream the veins
a deeper red than blood or life alone.
Shatter the self-hollow skeleton,
let me live new in You.
Speak your Word to live in me that I may echo,
Love, your melody.

VI.
Allelulia

Give Us This Day

Give us this day our daily bread
    not only food for body
    in our human need,
    but that living bread
    that embodies us
    and relates us to one another –
    those we love
    and those we should,
    those we know,
    those gone before us,
    those whose aching needs
    implore us to reach out
    and hold a hand we'd rather not
    but can't refuse
    if we'd be true to You.

Give us this day our daily bread
    by which we're healed,
    bread broken and shared,
    forgiveness sealed,
    and we are sent –
    a sacrament to a wanting world.

A Prayer for Bits and Pieces

"Come, O Holy Spirit, enkindle our hearts
with the fire of Thy divine Love..."

Let a bit of your love live here in my heart,
bright enough to calm the darkness within
and the darkness that surrounds us.

Give me a bit of your love and peace,
a vigil light of hope for change here and now,
a small steady flame to light another,
to be there for a sister or brother.

Give me a bit of your love and fortitude
enough to tame the shadows,
enough to safely walk through the dark night
into your rising Son on the edge of our world.

In Hopes of Hatching

I have confidence
that Christ who broke through death will
someday break through me.

$\mathcal{L}$ines in $\mathcal{H}$onor of One Who $\mathcal{L}$oves $\mathcal{M}$e

Oh, I love the things around me
and the things I cannot see
that speak so proud and loud of Thee.

I love the faint and feeble sign
of Omnipotence and Love divine.
I drink it in like rare good wine,

Sipping slow the dizzy taste
(careful not a drop to waste)
of Lover in the loved traced.

Of What to Sing in Spring

Shall I sing of wind and sun, oh,
shall I say how brightly blown
are the hopes of babe and bud so
tightly tender grown?

Shall I say of bush and tree then,
they grow all green anew,
sing last spring's song again
how this spring's mystery grew?

Shall I say that I am spring-free,
how spring-sweet is Thy song?
Or say how glad I have Thee
and how I've longed so long?

*L*ove

Love is not a mathematician.
Love is not calculated, timed, or spaced.
The thing of it is a welling up
and spilling over—
a noncontainment of filling
and overflow or burst.

Fatal to measure love,
to try to equalize
impossible and foolish
as limiting a butterfly to just
one flower.

Do not count the ways.
Do not ration me
or you.
Be all at the moment.
Don't punch clocks with me.
It is hard enough to know
the oh how long
and sweet enough
the sometime soon.

Don't be afraid of my tender.
Don't say no to my always.
Too soon enough come ebbs.
You have known the cold
and the dry winds of my emptiness.
To you the fullness (such as it is)
also belongs.

Lesson in the Labyrinth

There is a discipline in the path
and the process.
Time and speed do not matter,
but slower is better.
Resting is permitted,
reflection recommended
on the way and its windings
whether near or far from the Center.

The Center and circumference
are the only true landmarks.
Distance and direction are elusive
but deliberate, both inward and outward.
Both are necessary,
both demanding faithfulness to the journey.
Each has its blessing.

Darling, I Am Growing Older

When I was young I aged
year by year, another inch,
outgrew this and that,
another grade, another skill,
another chore at home.
I gloried in it!
Now that I'm old and gray,
I age day by day—
another pain, a slowing down.
It takes longer now
to clean the house,
to rake the leaves,
to recall a name.
It's there somewhere,
but words lag behind
my young-old mind
which inside me dances still,
wise and graceful.
I suppose that, too,
will slip away.
Until that time, I do
what I can today.
And glory in it!

Query

Someday we may be extinct as dinosaurs,
leaving traces in the sands piled up over hills
   and valleys
where we lived and left our mark,
not as indelibly as we may have believed.

What kind of end will it be?
Swift meteoric ball of flame?
Volcanic expulsions searing everything in its lava path,
suffocating in its toxic ash-filled cloud?
Will the end come slowly stifling ourselves
   with global warming
fed by our selfish excesses and greed that exploit
and annihilate even those living beings that sustain us?

Can we earn a millennium or two of peace and harmony
clothed in dignity and leanness of living
well within our means and within modes
respectfully recognizing the divine in all that is?
Will our end come gracefully, knowing and
acceding it is our time to go, fulfilled and finished,
one at last with all in our Eternal Source?

Remembering

To remember, to recall,
to bring to mind,
to find ourselves,
our weaknesses, our strengths,
our gifts, our flaws.

Remember to learn, to celebrate,
to discover wisdom in our days,
to savor the good,
to heal the sad,
to recognize the change,
to renew the heart and fire.

*A*ffirmation

Surely you've brought me
home to my heart which is just
a "we" bit of yours.

Our Journey's Landmarks

We tend to recognize landmarks
by chunks of time: five years, ten,
twenty-five, fifty, seventy-five.
But that is not how they are made,
that is not how they become alive.

Consider the minute minute. Glory in it.
Celebrate the mix of doubt and hope,
fear and courage, sickness and health,
poverty and wealth, good and bad
and all the in-between
the graying and the green.

Love is not just romance—
cherish the joy of song and dance,
but recognize the presence
along with the presents,
the care and the courtesies
born of love and discipline.
The constancy through grit and gory
are words behind the story
of the glory celebrated now.

Thank You Prayer

There are some days so good
I wonder how happiness could
happen to such a great degree
to simply plodding me.
I am thankful. My heart lifts,
but dare not ask for gifts.
Yet my beggarly heart is leaping.
These things are not in keeping
with the road I've trod.
I dare not dream my God
so lavish as to ravish the limits of my soul,
make my hurting spirit whole
if but for a day,
yet hope He may
again.
Amen.

Prayer to My Prodigal God

Have I told you lately that I love you?
And yet I know it's not as much
as you love me.
Have I thanked you for so graciously
listening to my complaints and demands
or thanked you for the multitude of lovely
gifts: the brilliant sunshine, the bird song,
the softness of snow, buds on the branch,
green things poking through in the garden,
a friend's call, unexpected letters,
community, little explosions of laughter,
opportunities to learn, and celebrious events?

Have I told you lately that I love you?
And yet I know it's not as much
as you love me.
Have I thanked you for strengthening me
with little sufferings and sorrows
and plenty of work to stretch my heart
to love a little more like yours?
Have I thanked you for the challenges,
the failures, the hopes, and the forgiveness,
the insights and the darkness
that help me see a little more like you?
Have I told you lately that I love you?
And yet I know it's not as much
as you love me.

*W*oman at the Well in Samaria

To be known down to the roots,
to be forgiven of all sin,
to be welcomed as beloved,
invited to enter within
the loving heart of God.
"Come, beloved Daughter.
Drink the Living Water."

This Is My Body

This is my body,
my not only flesh
and blood and bones—
my all of me,
the nothing more left
to lay out for you.
Take it,
ground and broken
out of my hands into yours,
life into love into life
for you.

*M*emorial

It's not so much the conscious monument,
the planned legacy,
as being merely what we are
and doing simply what we do
that leave the last-forever love prints.

Short Prayer

Lord, if you will not be
with me,
be at least with those
who love me.

Scriptural References in the Poems

A Feast of Angels Michael, Gabriel, Raphael
Luke Chapter 1: 26-38   *Tobot* Chapters 5 & 6

After the Angel *Luke* Chapter 1:25-26

Reflection on Annunciation *Luke* Chapter 1:25-26

Bethlehem Blessing *Luke* Chapter 2

Joan of Arc *Exodus* Chapters 3-14 (about Moses),
1 Samuel Chapter 17 (about David), *John* 10 (about
Jesus as Shepherd) and *John* 1:29 (about Jesus as
Lamb)

Dachau Now *Luke* Chapter 23:33-34

Ephesians *Ephesians* Chapter 2:19-22

Forgiveness *Genesis* Chapter 3

John the Baptist *Luke* Chapter 3, Mark 1:2-8

Magi Again *Matthew* Chapter 2:1-12

Magdalen Easter Morning *John* Chapter 19:25,
John Chapter 20:11-19

Night Prayer *John* 6:33-35

This Is My Body *Luke* Chapter 22: 14-20

Woman at the Well in Samaria *John* Chapter 4:4-30

Design: Todd Sanders, Publishing Services Group

Editor: Thomas Masloski, Siquis

Typesetter / Page Makeup: Todd Sanders

Headline font: 14 pt. Apple Chancery w / 24 pt. Apple Chancery Initial Cap

Text: 12/14 Times New Roman

Printer: CHG, Grand Rapids, MI